A Doll's House

Henrik Ibsen (1828–1906), Norwegian poet and playwright, was one of the shapers of modern theatre, who tempered naturalism with an understanding of social responsibility and individual psychology. His earliest major plays, *Brand* (1866) and *Peer Gynt* (1867), were large-scale verse dramas, but with *Pillars of the Community* (1877) he began to explore contemporary issues. There followed *A Doll's House* (1879), *Ghosts* (1881) and *An Enemy of the People* (1882). A richer understanding of the complexity of human impulses marks such later works as *The Wild Duck* (1885), *Rosmersholm* (1886), *Hedda Gabler* (1890) and *The Master Builder* (1892), while the imminence of mortality overshadows his last great plays, *John Gabriel Borkman* (1896) and *When We Dead Awaken* (1899).

Zinnie Harris's plays include the multi-award-winning *Further than the Furthest Thing*, produced by the National Theatre/Tron Theatre in 2000 (1999 Peggy Ramsay Playwriting Award, 2001 John Whiting Award, Edinburgh Festival Fringe First award); *Nightingale and Chase* (Royal Court Theatre, 2001); *By Many Wounds* (Hampstead Theatre, 1999); and *Silver Whale Fish* and *Master of the House* (BBC Radio Four). *Solstice*, the first in a trilogy of plays, was staged in 2005 by the RSC, who had already presented *Midwinter* in 2004; the last, *Fall*, was staged at the Traverse, Edinburgh, in 2008. Zinnie Harris had received an Arts Foundation Fellowship for playwriting, and was Writer in Residence at the RSC 2000–2001.

HENRIK IBSEN

A Doll's House

in a new version by
ZINNIE HARRIS

faber and faber

First published in 2009
by Faber and Faber Limited
74–77 Great Russell Street, London WC1B 3DA

Typeset by Country Setting, Kingsdown, Kent CT14 8ES
Printed and bound by CPI Antony Rowe, Chippenham, Wiltshire

A CIP record for this book
is available from the British Library

ISBN 978-0-571-24954-1

2 4 6 8 10 9 7 5 3

A Doll's House in this version was first performed at the Donmar Warehouse, London, on 14 May 2009. The cast was as follows:

Nora Gillian Anderson
Thomas Vaughan Toby Stephens
Christine Lyle Tara Fitzgerald
Dr Rank Anton Lesser
Neil Kelman Christopher Eccleston
Annie Maggie Wells

Director Kfir Yefet
Designer Anthony Ward
Lighting Designer Hugh Vanstone
Composer and Sound Designer Tim Phillips

Characters

Thomas Vaughan
a member of the cabinet

Nora Vaughan
his wife

Annie
their maid

Christine Lyle
an old friend of Nora's

Neil Kelman
a disgraced politician

Dr Rank
a friend and regular visitor to the house

Ivor *and* **Emmy**
the Vaughans' children

A DOLL'S HOUSE

Act One

London, December 1909. Christmas Eve.
  The drawing room of a large Victorian house.
  It's quite empty, apart from a few packing cases, a
chair or two covered in dust sheets and a Christmas tree.
  In the middle of the room stands a woman.
  The woman moves the Christmas tree to a spot by the
window.
  Then she stands back. She doesn't think it is quite in
the right place; she moves it again.
  It is quite an effort to move.
  She assesses the position: that is better, but not quite
right.
  She moves it again.
  Yes, now it is perfect.
  She takes a few bits of tinsel out of her pocket and
puts them on the tree.
  She giggles, delighted.
  A man's voice calls through the door.

Thomas Mouse?

Nora You can't come in.

Thomas Why ever not?

Nora I don't want you to see it until it's decorated.

Thomas I have seen a tree before.

Nora Not this one.
  I mean it – stay where you are.

Thomas So what do you suggest we do, talk through the
door?

Nora If you like.

Thomas Remind me, in this house, who are the adults and who are the children?

He comes in through the door.

Nora You ruined it.

Thomas I thought it was a joke.

Nora What do you want anyway, I thought you were working?

Thomas I can't find anything, everything's a mess.

Nora Oh.

Thomas Annie says there's a list somewhere that says what's what, but I can't even find the list, so really –

Nora What are you looking for?

Thomas Shirt cuffs. A collar.
A tie would be nice.

Nora The cases are all labelled.

Thomas I can't get at the cases for the piles of stuff that have come out of the cases.

Nora I'll get Annie on to it.

Thomas I hate moving house.

Nora Well, you can't come and decorate the tree.

Thomas Why not?

Nora You should be working.

Thomas It's Christmas Eve.

She puts a ribbon on the tree, looks at him.

Come on, one ribbon.

Nora You'll put it in an odd place.

Thomas I can be aesthetic.

Beat.

Where did they come from anyway?

Nora What?

Thomas The ribbons?

Nora The market.

Thomas And the bells?

Nora They were cheap.

Thomas We have decorations.

Nora We have old decorations that are half broken.

Thomas They functioned, they did what decorations are supposed to do.

Nora Thomas, really.

Thomas They hung there, where they were put.
They said hello, look at me, happy Christmas.

Nora That's why I don't let you decorate the tree.

Thomas What was wrong with them?

Nora They were ugly.

Thomas All decorations are ugly.

Nora How can you say that?

Thomas They're a gross misuse of money. They say look at me, I'm a waste of resources. I'm just here to cheer up a dead tree that's going to go out in the rubbish come January.

Beat.

Nora You don't think that.

Thomas I might.

Nora I know you don't.
   You love Christmas.
   You're just like the children, so excited for the morning you can't sleep the night before.

Thomas Am I?

Nora Yes. And you love decorations as much as I do.

   Beat.

Thomas What else did you get?

Nora Bits and bobs.

Thomas Oh?

Nora Essential things.
   This tree's going to be perfect.
   It looks like an illustration from a book, don't you think?
   Now you've seen it, you might as well comment.

   He looks at it.

Thomas So it does.

   Beat.

Nora I want everything to be just right, that's all.

Thomas It will be.

Nora But just a little more just right than last year, don't you agree?

Thomas Nora –

Nora Well, with our change in fortune.
   And this, this house will need a huge amount of decoration. It looks like no one's painted it for years, whoever the last inhabitant was –

Thomas Kelman.

Nora Kelman.

Thomas He was single.

Nora There we are then. No wonder it looks so drab.

Thomas My salary doesn't officially start until January, remember.

Nora But you're doing the work already.

Thomas Only because Kelman had to go so suddenly. And when you get to be appointed to a position like this –

Nora So are we supposed to borrow?

Thomas No, we're supposed to live within our means until then.

Nora I am.

Thomas Everything's up in the air, Nora, we just have to do what's expected of us.

Nora But when the pay cheque comes in, it will be huge –

Thomas But that's precisely my point, *when* it comes in. And it isn't in yet.

Nora They can't expect us to live in this dreary house without a little cheering it up for Christmas.

Thomas No, but we have to be moderate.

Nora That word again.

Thomas There's nothing wrong with moderation. Decorations yes, but last year's.

Nora Uggg.

Thomas A turkey but not a huge one, presents but no big surprises.

Nora Less joy on the children's faces.

Thomas Nonsense.

Nora Less delight at the beauty of the house.
Less laughter.

Thomas Not at all.

Nora Less treats.
More or less where we've always been in fact.
The land of moderation.

Thomas Just for a little longer.

Nora Or . . . we could take out just a little loan, for Christmas?

Beat.

Have a really wonderful time, enjoy ourselves.
Celebrate your success.

Thomas And what happens when something unforeseen occurs, when I accidentally step out in front of a tram?

Nora Don't be silly.

Thomas Before the first pay cheque even reaches the bank.

Nora It won't happen.

Thomas Then you'd be in debt, with no way to repay it.
Bankrupt.

Nora You have a very dark imagination.

Thomas I'm just saying it's particularly important that we're prudent, don't make any rash decisions. We're living in the public eye now, and that means we'll be under scrutiny all the time.

Nora I don't like it when you talk like that.

Thomas Like what?

Nora As if there's this eye, this great public eye that watches everything.

Thomas My sweet girl, not everything in this world is as lovely as you wish.

Beat.

Here.

He takes some money out of his wallet.

With my love.
And my knowledge of how all these essentials add up.

Nora Thank you.

She takes it.

How come you aren't working?

Thomas I couldn't find anything, I told you. I'd love to work if I could find my briefcase, my notes, a pencil would be nice.

Nora I'll get Annie on to it.

Thomas Later.
As you said, it's Christmas Eve.

Beat.

Come a little nearer to me.

She comes a little nearer.

You know your happiness is almost infectious, when you are around I feel it too.

Nora I'm so proud of you.

He takes her hands.

But you're cold.

Thomas No.

Nora Freezing.

Thomas I've just been sitting still.

Nora I'll tell Annie to light a fire.

Thomas She'll be busy with the children, don't worry her.

Nora raises an eyebrow, as if to query what he might be saying.

What?

She takes his hands, breathes on them.

How did I get a wife like you?

Nora You chose well.

Thomas Of course I did.

Nora So how warm exactly would you like to be?

Thomas Mrs Vaughan . . . ?

Nora I don't know what you mean!

Thomas I'm a member of the cabinet now. What if we were to be heard?

Nora We could be very quiet.

Thomas You're really quite something.

Nora As I say – just a suggestion.

Thomas It's an interesting one.

Nora Oh, you like it?
  The children are in the nursery doing what the children must do, the servants are downstairs already starting to think about dinner, the gardener is planting bulbs for the spring. The piano tuner is upstairs.
  All are doing as they must.

Thomas And we?

Nora My darling Thomas, it's Christmas Eve.

Thomas You know – you should have been the politician, you make quite an argument.

Pause.
  The bell rings.
  Pause.

Damn.

Nora Ignore it.

She brings his hands back up to her mouth.
  She breathes on them.

Annie will go.

Thomas But what if it's important?

Nora It's Christmas Eve.

Thomas In my post.

Nora I know – there's no such thing as being off duty.
  But today . . .

The doorbell rings again.

Thomas She isn't answering.

Nora She'll answer.
  We'll give her a stern talking-to later.
  But for the moment –

Thomas I'm just worried about who it will be.
  We don't want to keep anyone waiting on our doorstep.
  Unless it's the delivery boy.

Nora The delivery boy?

Thomas Could it be?

Nora I don't think so.

Thomas Are you sure? Think hard now.
I wouldn't mind, you know, if it was.
I would understand.

Nora Would you?

Thomas You spend money because it's your nature, it's very straightforward.
It's difficult for you to do anything else. Dangerous even.
A sheep must be as a sheep is.
A wolf as a wolf.
And my little Nora-mouse.
Maybe I should dress you in pound notes and be done with it. Sew you together a little outfit made out of nothing but paper. Hmm?

The bell rings again.

She hasn't answered, Nora.

Nora She'll be on her way.

Thomas Whoever it is will be standing in the cold, freezing.

Nora So let them freeze.
I'll talk to Annie later.
I'll chastise Annie later.
The little delivery boy can come back tomorrow.

Thomas So there is a delivery boy?

We hear Annie's voice through the door.

She's answering now.

Nora So she is.

They listen. Thomas's hands still on Nora's legs.

It is Christmas Eve, even God himself will have some time off, after all.

Annie A visitor for you, ma'am.

Nora For me?

Annie She says she has an appointment.

Nora Who is it?

Annie A Mrs Lyle.

Nora Is it three already?

Thomas Mrs who?

Nora Christine Lyle.
A friend of mine, I totally forgot.

Thomas So surely we can tell her to call tomorrow, whoever she is.

Nora Do your shirt back up, Thomas.

Thomas We are really going to be interrupted by a friend of yours?

Nora I have to talk to you about something.

Thomas You look serious.
How can my little mouse suddenly look so serious?

She smoothes out her clothing.

Nora Annie, please tell Mrs Lyle I'll be a few minutes. Tell her to take her coat off and warm herself by the fire in the library.
Indeed, I told her to come at three o'clock.

Thomas She'll understand.

Nora She hasn't got as much as we have and she'll have taken the tram from the other side of the city to get here.

Thomas Well, only fools travel by tram in London in the first place.

Nora Oh, she's no fool.

Thomas Nora, do we really have to talk about her now?

Nora She's an educated woman, Thomas.

Thomas It's Christmas Eve.

Nora In fact she's extremely intelligent. Resourceful, honest, hard-working.

Thomas Who is this woman?

Nora We were at school together.

Thomas She was at the same school as you?

Nora She listened harder than me.

Thomas You've never mentioned her.

Nora Haven't I?

Thomas I don't think so.

Nora That's strange because she was a very good friend. Well, we might have lost touch a little since then but at school we were inseparable.

Thomas I look forward to meeting her some *other* day.

Nora You'll be quite bowled over by her. Impressed, that's what you'll be.

Thomas Are you being serious?

Nora Deadly.

Thomas starts to wonder where this is headed.

Thomas Is this part of some performance, Nora? Some game you're playing?

Nora She was the one getting good marks, Thomas. Really. Impressing the teacher. You think you can count, you should meet Christine, the way she can add up, without any abacus or counting aid, faster than lightning, all the numbers whirring around in her head. And the way she can type.

She's quite something.

Thomas So you said.

Nora And she wants to meet you.

Well of course she does, I told her I had this clever, compassionate husband. Who of course has had a promotion.

Thomas Mouse, just say it.

Beat.

Nora All right, I'll say it.

Thomas She wants a job.

Nora Exactly.

Thomas In my office?

Nora Well she, she's looking for a man that she can really learn from, she's keen to learn, you see.

Thomas I wish you would just say this boldly, rather than all this going around the houses.

Nora It's in my nature.

Little Nora-mouse must squirrel and squeak.

Thomas She can type?

Nora Like the wind.

Thomas Fine. I'll see if I can give her a position. I can't make any promises, but if she's as good as you say she is . . .

Nora Oh, she's very good.

Thomas Then I'd be a fool not to employ her. Isn't that so?

Beat.

As it happens there may be a vacancy coming up soon,
I'll put her name forward. I still don't understand why
she must disturb us on this afternoon.

Beat.

Nora You want me to keep her waiting? Honestly?

Beat.

Thomas She is by the fire, after all.

Nora She got the tram.

Thomas She can take it back.

Nora She's a woman, Thomas, and she's come a long
way.

Thomas If she's as desperate as you say, another half-
hour won't kill her.

Nora She's a friend of mine.

Thomas And what about me?

Nora What do you mean?

Thomas What am I to you?

Nora Well of course you are my husband.

Beat.

Thomas You have no idea how important I am, do you?
It's almost quite sweet. The whole country is looking to me
now, as part of the cabinet. The economy is precarious,
the whole of Europe a tinderbox, and I am one of the
new government.
     Next to the Prime Minister I'm one of the most
important men in London. Last week I may have just
been another Member of Parliament, but now –

The bell rings.

All I'm saying is, many women would be glad to see their husbands on Christmas Eve, love to spend time with them and the children. Particularly a man who doesn't have much time to give.

Nora As you wish. I'll send her away.

Thomas There's so much work I'm swimming in it. Serious things, Nora, big decisions that I'll have to decide about. And the paperwork, after Christmas when the job really starts I'll be hardly ever with you.

Annie comes to the door.

Annie Someone else to see you, sir.

Thomas This could even be the Prime Minister now.

Nora Who is it, Annie?

Annie Dr Rank.

Nora You can keep Dr Rank waiting.
Annie, can you tell him to call back later?

Thomas No.
This is no way to treat our friends.
He's a man after all and no doubt he's also made the journey.

Nora Put him by the fire next to Christine – they can both wait.

Thomas I am sorry, Nora, Dr Rank has no doubt some business to discuss with me, and business comes first. You are edible, Nora, but even I must be careful not to feast too much.
Excuse me.

He begins to leave.
Beat.

Nora Thomas?

He stops.

I love you.

She rushes over to him.

I'll make it up to you.
    You'll get as much of me as you wish this Christmas.

Thomas I must see my visitor, Nora.

Nora Of course you must.

Thomas And you must understand how serious my work is, we must be sober about it. This is everything that I have worked for, Nora.

Thomas leaves.
    Nora by herself.
    She puts the money he gave her in her stocking.
    She takes a second to regain her composure.
    Then she goes to the door.

Nora Christine.

Christine comes in.

Christine My dear Nora.

Nora You look freezing.

Christine I'm fine now.
    I sat by your fire.

Nora Don't you have gloves?

Christine I took them off.

Nora Well put them back on, your fingers are quite blue.
    I know it's cold out there but this is ridiculous. Oh dear me.

Christine gets out her gloves.

She doesn't put them on.

Christine I'd prefer not to wear gloves in the house.

Nora What is this, superstition?

Christine No.

Nora Then let me see them.

Nora takes the gloves out and has a look.
They have holes in the fingers.
She gives them back to Christine without comment.

I have good news.

Christine He said yes?

Nora There's a vacancy, he'll put you forward.

Christine What does that mean?

Nora A formality only. He likes to be seen doing things the right way. Don't worry, it's a yes.

Christine Did you have to beg him?

Nora Of course not, he's a kind man and besides, I told him he'd be a fool not to have you. That you were exquisite at typing, and a thoroughly good thing. You *are* exquisite at typing, aren't you?

Christine Of course I am.

Nora Good.

Christine And I check and double check and when I get them wrong I always find my mistakes. You didn't tell him I was *too* good?

Beat.

Nora You'll be fine.

Christine Of course I will.

Nora A government clerk, how hard can it be?

Besides, you don't want to go around in gloves like that for the rest of your life, do you?

Christine gets something out of her bag.

Christine I nearly forgot.

She gives a bag of macaroons to Nora.

Payment. Glad to see some things never change.

Nora I'm only supposed to eat them occasionally.

Christine Really? I would have thought with all this money –

Nora He worries about my teeth.

Christine Oh.

Nora He likes me to have nice shining white teeth.

And slim hips.

He's more worried about the hips than the teeth if the truth be told. We had our photograph taken yesterday for the paper and he told me to stand sideways so I would look as slim as possible.

Christine Appearances are important.

Nora Of course they are.

I want slim hips too, God forbid to have a hide like an elephant, we're both interested in my having slim hips.

Christine puts the macaroons away.

Hey.

Christine I am not comfortable with this.

Nora Don't be such a fuddy-duddy.

Christine He has forbidden you.

Nora Not forbidden, no, he isn't that sort of man, just strongly recommended.

Christine If I am to work in his ministry, I would rather not start a working relationship on the basis of defiance. I should be loyal to him now.

Nora Oh just give them to me would you, Christine?

Christine gives Nora the macaroons.

Do you want one?
I don't mean to be rude but it's a little late to worry about your hips.

Christine laughs.
She eats one.

Take two.
We're going to have to finish the whole bag.

Christine takes two.
Nora takes three.

You're going to have to be my supplier, now that I've got you this job. You're going to have to smuggle them in.

Christine You're exactly the same, you know that.
This world is upside down and different, but you, you're completely the same.

Nora has crammed them into her mouth.

Nora And you too, and I can't tell you how happy I am.
We've been through some times, Christine, but now here, with this house and this new job – I'm starting to think that everything's been worth it.

Christine Strange isn't it, you seem to have changed not a stitch, and yet me?
When I look in the mirror I don't see myself staring back.

Nora Nonsense.

Christine You were polite yesterday, Nora, I know you were, but when I came to your door, you wouldn't have recognised me if I hadn't announced myself.
The years have not favoured me as much as you.

Nora I'm sorry, I shouldn't have spoken about myself so contentedly.

Christine Why shouldn't you?
After all you've had nothing to contend with.
Be content, Nora, enjoy it.

Nora I've had my share of hardship.

Christine What, the maid off sick, not enough money for macaroons?
Please, Nora, I don't want to argue, but don't make me laugh.

Nora You know very little about me.

Christine I know what I can see.
When my husband died I was left without anything.
And I mean anything, it was my own resilience that kept me from being destitute. In fact it was only because I was so glad to see the back of him that I kept going. Even working my fingers to the bone I counted myself fortunate that I'd got rid of the old sod.

Nora You can't mean that.

Christine I didn't marry for love, Nora, you know that.
I married because my mother was sick and I needed a man with an income.
Don't look shocked. You know nothing of my life.

Nora Nor you, of mine.

Beat.

Christine I'm sorry, I don't mean to quarrel, particularly after your kindness.

Nora I'm not as dim-witted as everyone thinks.

Christine Of course you're not.

Nora Thomas had a breakdown. I don't suppose you heard about it, it isn't mentioned here and no one knows. Even Thomas now won't let me talk about it. We hardly talk about the past at all. He lost his wits completely, if you want to know. Eight years ago, he went quite mad, Christine. Not the mad you've read about in books, mad ravings and screaming out in the night. No, just an exhausted, sad kind of mad that fills the days with tears.

You say I haven't seen hardship, and yes, I've never put a foot inside the poorhouse, but I have slept next to a man that for six months hardly recognised me and I him.

Christine It can't have been like that.

Nora It was worse.

If the maid talked to him, he could hardly understand. If a card came to the door, I had to read it for him and then send whoever it was away. Above all I had to keep him hidden. He'd just started in politics and I had to take him away before anyone found out how bad he was, or he would never get re-elected and we'd be finished. It was overwork, I'm quite sure of it. The doctor who examined him said that a rest was what he needed, and that I'd find he'd come back to himself little by little.

He'd just won his first seat. Out in the sticks, so I had to tell a few fibs, pretend that he'd caught pneumonia from walking house to house and canvassing.

Christine You told lies?

Nora I had to. That's why we went to Italy. Not exactly when we might have chosen to have an extended holiday, what with the twins newly born.

And it cost us dearly.

You want to know how much it cost? Twice the deposit we put on our house. We couldn't sell where we were, and we had to rent over there, quite apart from the cost involved in running two houses, and with no income.

Christine But your father has money.

Nora My father never saw Thomas in a good light. To ask him for money would have confirmed his suspicions. He always thought that politics was a vanity and I was determined that nobody would know the reason why we left for Italy, so I found it myself.

Christine How could you have?

Nora I told you, I'm not the silly Nora that everyone thinks I am.

Christine I owe you an apology. I feel we've quarrelled like schoolchildren.

Nora At least let me finish my tale now you've started me on this line.

Christine You don't need to convince me.

It's the worst of being me, I say things I only mean to think.

Nora How do you think I came by the money?

Christine I have no idea.

Nora What would you have done if you were in my shoes?

Christine I am not as resourceful as you, obviously –

Nora But you've already told me you are.

When you needed money, you turned to a man.

Christine No, Nora, don't tell me.

Nora A rich fanciful admirer.
  Why not?
  What else could I do?

Christine You were married.

Nora Exactly, and so I must save my husband.

Christine You took a lover?

  Beat.

Nora Really, Mrs Lyle, is that the time? Perhaps you need to be going back for your tram.

Christine Tell me . . .

Nora Look again at my face, and tell me I haven't changed.

  Christine looks.

I wish I could tell you that I sat on an old man's lap and gained his fortune. Just for the look on your face, I wish you could see yourself now.

  Beat.

I did what a man would have done.

Christine What do you mean?

Nora I borrowed it. The whole sum.

Christine That's impossible.

Nora I did.

Christine But you would have needed your husband's consent.

Nora Not so, it turns out. I found a way around it.

Christine What way?

Nora You must never tell Thomas of this, do you swear? In fact no one, I've so far never breathed a word of this out loud. This is my secret, Christine, for your ears only. Let's just say, it turns out if you know a thing or two about business, and you're prepared to think like a man, you can find a way around these things.

And so I did.

Thomas assumes the money was my inheritance, my father died at just about that time. But as it turned out, I inherited nothing, my father had lost the lot.

Christine You should tell Thomas.

Nora Why? He's a proud man, Christine, you'll learn that when you work for him. He doesn't like to owe anyone anything, least of all his wife.

Have another macaroon –

Christine I shouldn't.

Nora Oh for goodness sake.

They both eat another macaroon.

Really, take off that scandalised look, you're putting me off my biscuit.

Beat.

Christine Are you still in debt?

Nora Don't gasp. Debt isn't as bad as you think. Oh, Thomas says that the walls will fall in if you even think of borrowing some money, but really, you just borrow the money and you find a way to pay it back. Simple. Well, apart from the interest, as it turns out that is the demon. You must pay back more than you borrow, strangely it's true.

Christine But you have no money to pay it back.

Nora So that is where the clever Nora comes in.
I work, Christine.
Yes, surprising eh, but yes, I do.
I do things for people.

And before you ask what sort of things, I want you to clear your face of that disapproval, we've established that sometimes one does things to survive. Well, I too have had to survive.

I have an array of things I do for people. Let's leave it at that. I do things that make people happy, people who have very little in their lives and are glad to see me.

And I save, of course. A little of everything that Thomas gives me. I dress from second-hand clothes that some ladies throw out, I patch them up and no one would know. This blouse, for instance, cost me nothing at all, likewise the skirt. The only thing I'm wearing that has any value are these earrings that Thomas gave me.

Nora giggles.

Christine You wear other people's clothes?

Nora Not only that, but Thomas does too. He has no idea. Old suits of men who died of some ailment or other. He thinks I buy them new, but I get them from clothing sales put on to help the poor, then I clean them or mend them, I'm so good at mending with tiny invisible stitches you would never know.

He goes to parliament every day wearing a dead man's suit.

Christine I can't believe what I'm hearing.

Nora And the presents I bought today. Second-hand all of them, I buy up things that people are throwing out then I give them to a delivery boy to bring in as new. And I save the money I would have spent. You wouldn't believe how clever I am, he doesn't suspect a thing.

Christine I can't believe any of this.

Nora I'm twelve hundred pounds in debt, Christine. Or I was. I had to find it from somewhere. What, would you rather I had taken a lover? Would that be more acceptable?

Christine Of course not.

Nora I am attractive, after all, and believe me I've had offers. It would be the simplest thing in the world to find some old man who could write a cheque for the whole amount.

Christine I don't find any of this funny.

Nora It isn't funny, just because I'm laughing doesn't mean I find it funny.

Christine I am worried for you.

Nora Don't worry for me, I look exquisite in whatever I wear.

Christine I didn't mean that.

Nora I saved his life, and I'm proud of it.
   But you can see why I'm so glad to have my husband in a new job and to be looking forward to Christmas. I'm sorry if I offended you by my happiness, Christine, but I do feel that after all this time I deserve it.

   The bell rings.

Christine Perhaps I should go.

Nora It will be for Thomas.

Christine I have to get the tram.

   Nora takes out the money from her stocking.

Nora Here, take a taxi.

Christine I couldn't.

Nora I insist.

Christine No, you keep it, and buy yourself something new.

Nora I'm proud of what I've done, Christine. How many women can say that they've saved their husband's life?

Christine Put your money away.

Annie comes to the other side of the door.

Annie Excuse me, there's a gentleman here who says he wants to see your husband.

Nora Then show him in.

Annie But he's with Dr Rank and has asked not to be disturbed.

Nora Show him to the library then, please, Annie.

Annie The delivery boy has been, the library's full of boxes.

Nora Who is this gentleman?

A man in his late forties, Neil Kelman, walks in the door.

Neil Just an old friend, Mrs Vaughan.

Beat.

Nora Mr Kelman.

Beat.

Neil Are you going to ask me to come in and sit down, or should I stand on the threshold? My threshold, I should say. So glad to see you looking so comfortable already.

Nora Entirely up to you.
What are you doing here?

Neil Making sure that you've settled in, what else? I don't like what you've done with the hall, mind you.
Don't worry, it's your husband I am after, not you.

Nora But as you can see, he's not here.

Neil Indeed.

Beat.

My apologies then.

Neil Kelman bows and leaves.

Nora He has a nerve. You would think with all the scandal that he'd just go and hide his head in the sand, but coming here –
Another macaroon, Christine, and quickly.

Christine I knew that man.

Nora Poor you.

Christine His name wasn't always Kelman, was it?

Nora I don't know, I don't know anything about him.
Is it me or has it gone freezing in here? Shall I call Annie and get her to lay a fire?

Christine I heard he was married.

Nora Was – the poor woman had better sense than to do a long sentence with him and died early, it seems, leaving him with a couple of boys.

Someone raps at the door.

Please, I already told you there's no room for you in here to sit with us.

Dr Rank appears around the door.

Dr Rank But you told me I was always welcome.

Nora I'm sorry! Do come in.
Christine, this is our good friend Dr Rank.

Dr Rank We met as we came in.

Nora Of course you did.

Dr Rank We had an unexpected wait in the library.
We talked a little about life, as I recall.

Nora Oh?

Dr Rank Mrs Lole tells me she's looking for work.

Christine Lyle.

Dr Rank My apologies, Lyle.

Nora She's found it now.

Dr Rank Congratulations.

Christine Thank you.

Dr Rank We fell out, as I recall.

Nora You mustn't mind Dr Rank, Christine, you'll get used to his ways.

Christine I didn't mind him a bit.

Dr Rank No indeed, we had a regular disagreement.

Christine Indeed we did.

Dr Rank She's quite the socialist, Nora, this friend of yours, she thinks we must hold out our hands to the morally corrupt, the sick, the indecent and find some nice well-paid job to install them in.

Christine I didn't exactly say that.

Dr Rank It was something along those lines, perhaps not exactly those words.

Christine I just said we must help those in most need of it.

Dr Rank Precisely, that was precisely what you said. And that's why women should never get the vote, they'd vote with their hearts not their heads in my opinion.

Christine I'll pretend I didn't hear that.

Dr Rank Shall I say it again a little louder?

Nora Macaroon?

Beat.

Dr Rank The library was warm enough, anyway, if a little frosty.

Nora Take two.

Rank takes two.

Dr Rank I thought they were forbidden?

Nora Kelman was here.

Dr Rank I saw. He's going to be a thorn in your husband's side, that one.

Nora I don't see what he wants here, there's no possibility of getting his seat back.

Dr Rank Men like Kelman don't lie down easily though, you know that. Where else has he got to go?

Christine He has two boys to support.

Dr Rank He should have thought about that before getting involved in the whole business. Thomas will see him off, anyway. There's nothing else to it.

Beat.

Christine I thought nothing was proved.

Dr Rank Oh, so you read the papers?

Christine Of course I do.

Dr Rank Quite the sophisticate.

Christine It's all allegation.

Dr Rank Allegation with credible witnesses.
The people he associated with.

Christine But until anything is proved –

Dr Rank He should be out of office.

Christine Innocent until proved otherwise?

Dr Rank For members of the public maybe, but members of Her Majesty's Government?
Ach, he was a soft-headed man and no one liked him.

Christine So it's fair?

Dr Rank In politics, yes.

Christine I think we might disagree again, Mr Rank.

Dr Rank I agree, I think we might. Jolly good.

Nora Another macaroon?

Christine I should be leaving, Nora, thank you so much for seeing me.

Nora Nonsense, he's only teasing.

Dr Rank I'm not teasing, I am quite serious.
I would dance on that man's grave.

Nora laughs.

Christine I don't see why someone's misfortune is a cause for celebration, that's all I'm saying.

Beat.
Thomas calls.

Thomas Nora-mouse?

Nora Here I am.

Nora rushes to the bag of macaroons and hides them away.

Thomas There you are.
Kelman was here.

Dr Rank We saw.

Thomas I can't believe that man, to come here and show his face –

Dr Rank It's incredible.

Thomas My words exactly.

Nora Thomas, this is Christine Lyle.

Thomas Ah, so this is she.
   My potential new clerk.

Christine I'm so dreadfully grateful.

Thomas Nonsense – Nora tells me you're an excellent asset.

Christine I believe I can be.

Thomas Then we'll have no more of this gratitude, your thanks will be in your work. There are some formalities but basically you came at a good time. Perhaps you can help me a little with my wife too.

Christine Your wife?

Thomas I think she eats too many macaroons.

Christine Macaroons?

Thomas Yes, and then she hides them from me.

   He finds the macaroons under a cushion.

Perhaps you can help me to make sure she refrains.

Nora Oh tsk.

Thomas Your teeth, Nora.

Nora I've been eating macaroons all my life, and look: they sparkle.

Thomas Really. Dr Rank, is there anything you can suggest for such a one?

Dr Rank All my suggestions proved ineffective long ago.

Nora You see what I have to put up with?

Christine laughs.

Thomas Now Nora, unfortunately I am going to have to go out for a short while.

Nora What about the tree?

Thomas When I get back.

Nora If you want.

Christine I too should leave.

Thomas Well then, let's walk down the road together, you can tell me a little of your experience up to this point.

Christine Certainly.

Christine kisses her friend.

Take care, sweetheart.

Nora See you soon.
      (*To Dr Rank.*) You'll stay a minute.

Dr Rank If you'll have me.

Nora Tell Annie to bring the children in.

Thomas The children? Dr Rank, can you bear it?
      This place will become a den of affection any moment, don't say I didn't warn you . . .!

Thomas and Christine leave.

Nora How are you?

Dr Rank A little worse, I think.

Nora The pain?

Dr Rank Don't worry about the pain.
      Many suffer worse than me.

Nora You said it takes your breath away.

Dr Rank Not when I'm distracted. When I'm with others I forget it.

Nora Well then, forget it now.

Dr Rank Exactly as I intend.

Annie brings the children in.
Nora gathers them up.

Emmy Mummy.

Nora Hello, darlings. Come here, Ivor.

She kisses them both.

Emmy, have you got a hello for Dr Rank?

Dr Rank Oh, don't make them.

Nora What about a smile then?
You should see her smile, really it'll brighten your day. Go on, Emmy. What about you then, Ivor, you can't be shy too? No I don't believe it, not shy? Hey? What do you think, Dr Rank, do you have any remedy for shyness in your doctor's bag?

Dr Rank Shyness. Ah, now that is a complicated affliction.

Nora Must we give them horrible-tasting medicine?

Dr Rank I don't think that's the treatment, no.

Nora What then, an injection?
With a large needle.

Dr Rank I don't think I've heard it cured that way.

Nora Or a little tablet?

Dr Rank No, here I have a remedy, I remember now.

Nora What is it, what is it?

Dr Rank It's quite wriggly.

Nora Wriggly?

This makes the children giggle.

Dr Rank Can I pass it to you?

Nora Where must I put it?

Dr Rank On their tummies and under their arms.

Dr Rank pretends to pass Nora something for the children.
  Nora carefully carries it over, then tickles the children.
  They squeal in delight.

There we are, my dear, quite cured.

Nora and the children squirm around, Nora letting them crawl all over her and tickle her back.

Nora Thank heavens for that. And so I see.

Emmy stops squirming, with news to impart.

Emmy Mummy, Ivor got his boot stuck in a grate and it was really funny.

Nora You didn't?

Emmy Annie and me had to pull him to get him out.

Ivor It's not funny.

Emmy Everyone was staring and he was like a great turnip and we were the farmers. He was really stuck.

Nora and Emmy giggle.

Ivor It's not funny at all.

Emmy Then when we got him out he fell into the mud, his face looked like a speckled egg. Splat.

Even Ivor giggles at this.

Nora Poor Ivor.

Emmy Or an old witch covered in warts.

Nora Show me how you fell.

Ivor Splat.

Emmy Splat splat.

The scene is relived, to much merriment.

Nora Splat splat.

Even Dr Rank laughs.
Kelman appears at the door.

Come here, see if I can pull you both like a turnip.

Nora is still squirming with the children.
Dr Rank stands up.
Nora stops.
The children sense their mother's tension.

Nora My husband is out.

Neil I didn't come to see your husband.

Nora No?

Neil Not this time. I realised there was something I'd forgotten to say to you.

Nora Me?
Can't you see I'm busy with my children?

Neil It really is most urgent.

Dr Rank For heaven's sake, man, there can't be anything you have to say to her. Your quarrel is with her husband.

Neil That's true, but I do wish a word with Mrs Vaughan.

Dr Rank It's intolerable, your being here at all, let alone this – get back out in the gutter and be done with you.

Emmy Who is he, Mummy?

Nora Dr Rank, would you be so kind as to take the children back up to the nursery.

Dr Rank You aren't going to see this man, are you?

Nora Two minutes.

Dr Rank I can't let you.

Nora He's quite harmless.

Dr Rank He's a rogue.
And a politician and I don't know which is worse.

Nora I'm sure I can manage him.

Dr Rank Nora, I'm serious.

Nora What harm can he do me, really?
You'll be right there, I could call.

Neil I only want a word.

Dr Rank Don't say anything, this is not a favour for you.

He looks from Kelman to Nora.

Are you sure?

Nora Quite sure.

Dr Rank gets up.
He takes the children by the hand.

Dr Rank Come on, Emmy, Ivor, let's go and see this famous boot that got stuck. Take me to the scene.

Nora I'll be up later, children, off you go.

They leave. Kelman and Nora are alone.

Are you completely mad?

Neil The papers seem to say I am.

Nora What on earth are you doing here?

Neil This is my house, Mrs Vaughan.

Nora It belongs to the government.

Neil Your husband is in my job.

Nora That is no concern of mine.

Beat.

It's the twenty-fourth.
    I have another week, eight days until the first.

Neil I haven't come about the money.

Nora So what on earth do you want with me?

Neil It hasn't been an easy week, Mrs Vaughan, as I'm
sure you can appreciate. This whole thing blew up out of
nowhere. Last week, ten days ago, I was getting on with
my life, looking forward to the New Year.
    My boys are nearly men.
    There was some praise in the House for a report I'd
just put in.
    I am good at my job, Mrs Vaughan.
    I have always been honest with the public.

Nora I am sure you have.

Neil Please.
    I can see the look you give me, you believe it just as
much as the next man.

Nora I don't read the papers.

Neil Well, you should. And you should watch out because
one day they might say the same things about you.
    I quarrelled with the Prime Minister – you want to
know what this is about, well I'll tell you. I didn't agree
with him on everything and I was prepared to say so. Big

40

mistake. Suddenly out of the past come all these things. Accusations. Old old things. Misdemeanours, yes, but small in the grand scheme of things. Tiny. But suddenly there they are in front of you and if you try to sidestep them or find another way around –

I love my job, Mrs Vaughan. I have always loved this job.

And actually I'm too good at it to be cast aside without another chance.

Nora What do you want from me?

Neil I want your husband to come out in the press on my side.

Nora What?

Neil Oh, I'm not naive, I know the game is up, I won't be back in my old seat, but he has influence now. With the cabinet as much as the electorate. If he were to say anything positive about me, even moderate, it would be listened to. Just enough to cast doubt on the allegations. I could leave it a few months, then start to crawl back.

Nora I don't have any influence with my husband.

Neil I saw him just now walking up the street with a woman.

Nora So?

Neil He is giving her a job, isn't he? I overheard them talking.

Beat.

Nora Well, since you ask so directly, yes.

Neil Simply because you and she are friends?

Nora I put a good word in and he listened, nothing is certain.

Neil Don't underestimate yourself. I think it was more than a good word, and why not? Why shouldn't he listen to his wife? It makes good sense.

Beat.

Nora You're mistaken if you think –

Neil I will not lose everything I've worked for, Mrs Vaughan, not because this rotten government grew tired of me. All I'm asking for is a few moderate sentences, a soothing whisper, some oil poured on this wound. It's lies they are telling about me, Mrs Vaughan, you understand that? How hard can a few sentences be?

Nora My husband is a difficult man.

Neil I know all about your husband.

Nora I don't think I can . . .

Neil I'm begging you, yes I am not afraid to beg.
A few sentences, after all.
That's all I want. A chance to climb back up.
I know your husband from when we were both students, and I know he can have his mind changed by a woman just as easily as the next man.

Nora I don't know what you're implying.

Neil Really? I would have thought a woman like you would know all about using her charms.

Nora You speak like that again to me and I'll show you the door.

Neil Courage. I like it.

Nora I am not frightened of you, Mr Kelman.
I'm one payment off never having to see your face again.

Neil But one payment is one payment. We're not finished yet.

I wish it didn't have to come to this, I wish I could have just said my piece and persuaded you how important your intervention is, but it seems you need a little more persuading, so here it is.

Nora Don't tell me you're going to tell my husband.

Neil That's one option.

Nora It would destroy him, you know that.

Neil I doubt it.

Nora He doesn't like secrets, you don't understand what it would mean.

Neil I am on the bottom rung of a ladder, there's only you between me and the gutter.

Nora Tell him then, I don't care. He would see you for what you are, and knock you clean into the mud.

Neil What about the papers then?

Nora What papers?

Neil The newspapers. Can you imagine the scandal?

Nora I don't think anyone would really be that interested.

Neil On the contrary, I think an awful lot of people would be very interested. Or perhaps it's directly to the law courts I should take it first?

Nora Law courts, whatever do you mean?

Neil You must have forgotten the details of the transaction that passed between us.

Nora I think of very little else.

Neil Let me remind you.

Nora It was a straightforward loan.

Neil Not quite. When Thomas was ill you came to me for some money, yes.

Nora Only because I had no choice.

Neil I found you the money, not my own, but I acted as an intermediary and asked no questions. You were the wife of a colleague and I could see you needed help. The only condition I had was that the loan was secured in some way. Now, the house wasn't in your name, in fact you had no collateral, so we needed your husband's signature. But you told me straight away that your husband would never sign as guarantor, indeed even the mention of a loan would be bound to make him sicker than he already was. And perhaps against my better judgement I took your word for it. I could have just turned my back on you, but I didn't – possibly because I was sympathetic to your plight or perhaps for my own reasons, however I did need someone to sign as guarantor, so I sent you an IOU.

Nora Which I signed.

Neil Of course you did, but underneath was another line, which was for your father to sign.

Nora Was to . . .? He did sign it.

Neil I left the date blank. Your father was to fill it in, remember?

Nora Of course.

Neil And I gave you the IOU to post to your father.

Nora Which I did.

Neil And about five or six days later you brought it back to me. I then, as promised, paid out the money.

Nora Is there a problem with the payments? We both know I haven't defaulted.

Neil It just leaves a small matter.

Nora What matter is that?

Neil Of your father, and his curious apparition.

Nora What apparition is that?

Neil Your father was quite unwell during this period, is that not right?

Nora I fail to see where this –

Neil When exactly did he die?

Nora 29th of September.

Neil Which is why the only explanation for events is that he appeared as a deathly incarnation.

Nora I don't follow you.

Neil Your IOU is signed and dated by your father, 2nd of October. Pretty odd.
     Now of course one explanation is that he signed but forgot to date it and you added that in later, and indeed that could be entirely appropriate, it doesn't really matter who dated it, because according to law it only matters who signed it.

Beat.

Nora Well, are you going to go on to accuse me?

Neil Must I accuse you?

Nora I think you already have.

Neil It is for your conscience, Mrs Vaughan.

Nora My father was ill.

Neil We've established that.

Nora It isn't the sort of thing to bother an ill man with.

Neil So maybe you shouldn't have gone on the trip.

45

Nora That was also impossible.

Neil Poor thing, caught in the middle then.

Nora I'm not ashamed of what I did.

Neil It's fraud.

Nora I was saving my husband's life, his reputation, his job.

Neil Fraud is what the papers will call it.

Nora What do you mean, 'will'?

Beat.

Neil That's up to you.

Nora I was saving a person's life.

Neil The press takes no account of motives.

Nora Then the press is misguided. Yes, I was trapped, between a dying father and a very sick husband, as the only person who loved them both I did what I could. I did what I had to, and if that makes me guilty of something, then fine, I'll stand for judgement. But I can't imagine a person in the land would condemn me.

Neil Then you know nothing of people.
    Let's hope it stays that way, Mrs Vaughan. No one would be interested if you were a regular housewife, but the wife of a cabinet minister, and involved in fraud?

Nora I have no influence with my husband.

Neil Then work out how to get some.
    Good day to you.

Kelman is gone.
    Nora sits down.
    She puts her head in her hands.
    Emmy appears at the doorway.

46

Emmy Mummy?

Nora doesn't move.
   Emmy comes over to her.

Mummy?

Nora Yes, sweet?

Emmy Will you come and play our game? Dr Rank is playing soldiers with Ivor and they're pulling their heads off.

Nora In a minute.

Emmy Who was that man?

Nora No one particularly important.

Emmy Does Daddy know him?

Nora Yes, but he makes your daddy cross. Don't mention him.

Emmy Why not?

Nora Because I'm asking you not to. Because sometimes, we girls must have a little secret between ourselves. Away from the boys.

Emmy Oh.

Nora That's what being a grown-up woman is. You'll find that out.

Emmy Will you still love me when I'm grown up?

Nora Of course I will.

Nora kisses her.

I'll love you even more for being grown up. One day. Now go back upstairs, Emmy, I'll be right up.

Annie comes in.

Annie.

47

Annie The delivery man is here again, ma'am.

Nora Heavens.

Annie He seems to have a lot of boxes.

Nora Then tell him to bring them in. Of course he must
bring them in.
  Off you go, Emmy.

Emmy goes.
  The delivery boy brings in boxes.
  Nora watches.
  More and more boxes.
  She stands up.
  Thomas comes in.

Thomas Back at last.
  Anyone here?

Nora No, just the delivery boy.

Thomas The delivery boy?

Nora Please, Thomas, I think I have a headache coming.
Yes, more boxes, but only essentials.

Thomas And someone else.

Nora I don't think so.

Thomas Not telling fibs are you, Nora? Not singing out
of tune?

Nora I can't recall any.

Thomas Really, Nora, I just saw Kelman this minute
walking out of the gate. I passed him on the path, he's
hanging around here like a ghost.

Nora Oh.

Thomas What's going on?

Nora Nothing.

Thomas Don't tell me he started plaguing you with tales of his innocence?

Beat.

That contemptible man.

Nora He has two boys.

Thomas Nora, really. What on earth possessed you to even talk to him? And then on top to tell me a lie.

Nora Not really a lie.

Thomas Yes, you said no one was here.

Beat.

A lie is a lie, Nora, however small.

Nora He's lost everything, Thomas.

Thomas Nora! Enough.
I absolutely forbid you to say any more.

Nora And it's all just allegation, nothing has been –

Thomas Enough!
He decided to become a politician, he knew how it works.

Pause.

I had an interesting conversation with Mrs Sylvester yesterday.
I think this will change your mind of it.

Nora Oh.

Thomas She was wondering if we'd be having a gathering like last year.

Nora A gathering.

Thomas She said it would be very seemly, for Boxing Day.
   Everyone enjoys our gatherings, and now we're in this post –

Nora If you like.

Thomas I thought it was a good idea. Celebrate our arrival.
   And you could wear fancy dress, Nora, just like last year.
   You can count on the Sylvesters to make good suggestions.
   And you so enjoy dressing up.

Nora Do I?

Thomas Come on, don't take that tone with me. You'll love it, I've already spoken to Annie and the staff about it. I was waiting to surprise you. You can dance and everyone will be charmed. Just like last year, yes?

   Nora nods.

Wonderful.
   Hey, little mouse. A smile?

   She smiles.

We've got a lovely Christmas ahead. The best.
   We will try not to fill it with work, and enjoy ourselves.

   She nods.

Nora But can I just ask, was it really something so terrible that Kelman did?

Thomas Nora, I've just said no more.

Nora I can read it for myself in the papers.

Thomas You've never shown any interest in the papers.

Nora I'll call for one tomorrow.

Thomas Fraud.
  If you want to know.
  That's what he did.

Nora That was all.

Thomas That was all? How can you say that?

Nora Maybe it was a mistake.

Thomas I dare say it was.

Nora Maybe he had no choice, I mean.

Thomas Everyone has a choice. However bad it gets, you always have the choice. Or even, yes, fine, I can conceive of a situation where one feels they have no choice, but afterwards, you should then be bold enough, remorseful enough, to admit guilt and take the punishment. But this man, he went on covering up his crime, until the circle of deceit just got worse and worse –

Nora How much worse?

Thomas Much much worse. Of course it did because, Nora, that's how fraud and deception works. It starts out with a small misdemeanour, perhaps not so dreadful in the grand scheme of things, but it's in the covering up, the secrecy required to maintain that discretion that the deception grows until, my dear, it has the perpetrator by the throat and there is no way back. That's why of all crimes I fear fraud the most. It always leads to a court case and a throttled man.
  And as a politician, our staple is trust. That is, after all, all we have to give to the public.
  And he lost it.

Nora How dreadful.

Thomas But the children, his children, that is the worst of it. On a human level.

Nora Why the worst?

Thomas Children are like little sponges, they absorb what's around them. And if what is around them is deceit and lies, then what else will become of them?

Nora Are you sure?

Thomas Kelman's boys will already be on the road to moral ruin, there is no question.

Nora No?

Thomas What chance did they have really?
    Exposed to all those lies on a daily basis. Thinking your parent to be one thing, only to find out they're another? A child can't survive that. Not really. It seeps into their blood through the atmosphere of the house. The lies of a parent, there is nothing so destructive really. How can a child believe or know what's true ever again?

    Nora gasps.

Hey, but no more.
    Now enough of this talk of men like Kelman, let's enjoy Christmas, eh?

Act Two

Christmas Day. The drawing room looks less bare now, more homely. The servants have unpacked some of the boxes overnight.

Annie and the children are in the drawing room, waiting.

Ivor is playing with a gun, Emmy with her new doll. Annie is standing.

Nora comes in but stays by the door.

Emmy rushes to her.

Nora pushes her off, gently.

Emmy What's wrong?

Nora Annie, I won't be seeing the children today.

Emmy Mummy?

Nora Would you mind taking them back upstairs?

Annie Of course.

Emmy Have we done something wrong?

Nora Now. If you wouldn't mind, Annie.

Annie I'd thought you'd be taking tea as usual.

Nora There are going to be a few changes to our schedule.

Emmy Mummy?

Nora Stay away, and don't cry, Emmy, please.

Emmy Is this about the secret?

Nora No, Emmy, there are no secrets now.

Emmy You told me there was a secret.

Nora Then that was wrong of me.
Secrets are very wrong, you understand?
Ivor, do as Annie says.
Don't touch me, I don't want you to come too near me.
Stay upstairs with Annie, she'll keep you safe.

Ivor I want to play with you.

Nora Not today, Ivor. I am no good for you today.

Ivor and Annie start to leave, Ivor holds on.

Ivor, please let go.
Ivor.

Annie comes back and pulls Ivor off.
  Ivor starts to cry.

It's better that you spend more time with other people,
for your own good.

All three of them go.
  Nora leans against the door.
  Oh God, is she doing the right thing?
  She picks up Emmy's doll.
  Sits it on a chair.
  Strokes its hair.
  Mrs Lyle comes in.

Christine The door was open.

Nora wipes a tear.

Whatever's the matter?

Nora Nothing.

Christine Your children are calling for you.

Nora That is the matter.

Christine Well get them down here, for goodness sake, it
is Christmas Day.

Nora No.

Please, Christine, no.

Christine I've never seen you like this.

Nora I think I influence my children too much.

Christine And what's wrong with that?

Nora You'll know soon enough.

Christine Nora?

Nora Please, I can't talk of it. If nothing else the children are too dependent on me, and it'll do them good to get used to other people. Who knows what will happen in the future, after all?

Christine Yesterday you were full of your new life and the children, but today –

Nora There is a world of difference between yesterday and today.

Christine When we were at school we would tell each other everything.

Nora I need to fix up this costume and then try it on. Oh God, no.

Nora looks out of the window.

Sorry, I thought there was someone coming up the path.

Christine And was there?

Nora No.

Christine You seem very jumpy.

Nora Pass the macaroons.

Christine I could only get a quarter.

Nora Then I'll eat a quarter.

Christine passes them.
    Nora throws her head back and tips in all the macaroons. She then screws up the bag and tucks it under a cushion.

Why only a quarter?

Christine That was all they had.

Nora You're supposed to be my supplier.

Christine I think we should call for some tea.

Nora I don't want tea.
    I want macaroons, that is why I asked you here.

Christine You seem out of sorts, are you brewing something?

    Nora laughs.

Nora Yes, I'm brewing something.

Christine Heavens, you aren't pregnant are you?

Nora No, nothing like that.

Christine I think you associate with the wrong people.

Nora Do you really?

Christine I have to say I don't think much of that Dr Rank, I think you see far too much of him.

    Nora laughs again.

Nora He's my little furry friend.

Christine That's what I mean, you shouldn't even think of a man like that.

Nora As a friend?

    Beat.

Christine Has Dr Rank money?

Nora Yes.

Christine Lots?

Nora I think so.

Christine I knew it.

Nora What did you know?

Christine Yesterday you were talking about an admirer, a lover even, as if it were something to be fooled around with. And then today, standing by the window, waiting for someone, not seeing the children, and he comes to the house every day, you said yourself.

Nora Please don't make me laugh.

Christine You may have started out with principles but that contemptible man . . .

Nora Dr Rank?

Christine Yes.

Nora laughs again.

Did he or did he not lend you that money?

Beat.

Nora You know, if he had been in a position to lend it to me, then I might well have asked him for it, and you know he's such a gentlemen, yes, a good and dear friend, he would have lent it to me without wanting anything in return.

Christine I can hardly believe that.

Nora He does love me, Christine and I him, but not in the way you imagine. Not in a way you can even conceive.

Christine And what way is that then?

57

Nora The way that's about two people admiring each other, as fellow travellers on this planet, not wanting anything other than friendship –

Christine You have no idea about men, do you?

Nora I have lots of ideas about men.

Christine Sometimes, Nora, I think you've hardly been out in the world.

Nora Have you lived a very hard life, Christine?

Christine We aren't talking about me.

Nora I don't know why we're talking at all.

Christine He said himself he didn't believe in charity.

Nora Who?

Christine Dr Rank.

Nora He wasn't talking about helping a friend.

Christine He'll want more and more of you, Nora.

Nora He didn't lend me the money.
Can't you hear?
HE DIDN'T LEND ME THE MONEY.

Christine You don't need to shout.

Beat.

I don't like the way he limps.

Nora He has tuberculosis of the spine.
OF COURSE HE LIMPS.

Beat.

Christine Whatever's got into you today?
There's more to this than too many macaroons.

Nora Tell me, if you've borrowed money and you pay it all back, do you get your IOU back?

Christine I expect so, yes.

Nora Have you any money I could borrow, Christine?

Christine Nora?

Nora It's a straightforward question.

Christine No. I have nothing. You know that.

Nora Damn.

Nora looks out of the window again.

Christine I can still hear the children.

Nora Can you? I can't.

Christine They're calling for you.

Nora That's my husband coming in now, he doesn't like to see mending lying about. Why don't you take it in to the children and get Annie to fix it up. Emmy loves dressing up.

Christine Why don't you come too?

Nora I will, in a minute.

Christine You can't just push me away, Nora, I know there's more to this.
  Whatever is going on?

Nora I just need to talk to my husband alone.
  Please, Christine, I have helped you.

Christine goes out of one door.
  Nora, alone for a second, bites her lip.
  She stands and brushes the crumbs off her lap.
  Thomas comes in the other door.

Thomas Cheer me up.

Nora Why do you need cheering?

Thomas I'm just discovering more and more about what went on in the department before me. It really amazes me, Nora, it really does.

Nora We've found my costume, from last year.
That's good news, isn't it?

Thomas Heavenly.
That is heavenly news.

He sits down.

Oh I do so love spending time with you. Your perspective on life is so refreshing. The news of the day – your costume is found. I love it. Tell me other things, how is the tree?

Nora Fine.

Thomas Great.
The little decorations, are they sparkling?

She takes his shoes off.
Starts rubbing his feet.

Nora Thomas.

Thomas Yes.

Nora Can I talk to you about something?

Thomas Don't tell me – you've bought a fancy fairy for the top?

Nora No.

Beat.

Thomas Why the serious look?

Nora I need to ask you something.

Thomas Oh?

Nora And I want you to say yes.

Thomas Whatever it is?

Nora Yes.
And then I'll make this Christmas more happy than –

Thomas I can't say yes whatever it is.

Nora Not even if I ask extra nicely?

Beat.

Thomas It doesn't matter how things are asked for, it is what it *is* that is important.

Nora Doesn't it matter just a little bit?

Beat.

Thomas Well, a bit perhaps.

Pause.

Is that it? No more questions?

Nora I just wondered.

Beat.

Thomas Well, now you have my attention you might as well come out and ask it.

Nora I'm worried about what you'll say.

Thomas Well, you shall have to ask all the more pleasantly.

Nora It concerns Kelman.

Thomas So you mean to make me angry?

Nora No.

Thomas Forget all about it, Nora.

Nora I just want to say one thing.

Thomas Forget it, I said.
Goodness, and I came in here to be cheered up.

Beat.

I understand you have some regret about the way I got this job.

Nora I thought you were innocent until proven guilty in this country.

Thomas The case against him –

Nora Could still collapse.

Thomas What on earth are you getting at, Nora? What on earth do you have in your head? The man is a liar, Nora, a cheat and a fraud.

Nora But he has nothing now.

Thomas So? What is this, charity?

Nora You could make a statement in the press. Or in the Commons. Even just privately amongst your friends. Pour some cooling water over the allegations. Just give him the possibility of a future, at some later date.

Thomas But why would I do that?
    Why on earth would I do that?

Nora He scares me.

Thomas I should take a stick to him for coming here at all.

Nora I think he means us ill.

Thomas I am sure he does.
    But what harm can he do us?

Nora He could make something up and put it in the papers.

Thomas But it wouldn't be true.

Nora It wouldn't matter if there was an allegation.
    It's only taken an allegation for his downfall, after all.

Thomas He's different to us.

He hasn't always conducted himself in the right way, and there are plenty that are glad to see him go. But us? I've always been righteous and moral.

Nora He'll accuse us of something, I know he will.

Thomas So let him try.

Nora But what if he finds something, some scrap of truth, and twists it?

Thomas I understand that you find political life precarious, but really, Nora, don't worry. I have a solid career behind me, I am well liked. There is nothing to taint us. We are secure in a way that he wasn't.

Nora Would a sentence or two from you be so hard to give?

Thomas Of course it wouldn't.

Nora It would be an act of charity. To be the only voice keeping an open mind.

Thomas In fact, Nora, I have in my bag the very same. I have written an article for a political journal about his behaviour and I am just about to send it to the press. It is very even, very level-headed.

Nora Can I read it?

Thomas Of course you can.

And everyone expects a statement from me in tomorrow's *Times*.

He hands it to her.
She reads it.

Nora It's vitriolic.

Thomas It is the truth as I see it.

Nora rips it up.

Whatever has got into you?
STOP IT.

Nora You can't send it.
You can't say these things.

Thomas grabs her by the arm.

Thomas And you can't get involved in my affairs like this.

He shakes her.

You're acting out of turn.
This is men's business, Nora.

He picks up the pieces.

Annie.

Nora I'm begging you.

Thomas ANNIE.

Nora Please, put it in the fire.

Thomas Wherever is she?

He rings the bell.

Nora Think of me, think of the children.

Thomas That is exactly what I'm doing.

Annie comes in.

Take these please and ask Mr McGuire to type them up afresh and send them straight over to Fleet Street. The name is on the top. Oh, and perhaps you could ask for a copy to be delivered to Kelman's new address.

Nora NO.

Annie Very good.

Thomas I will put a stop to that man and his lies, Nora.

Nora is still on the floor.
Thomas is furious.
Beat.

How do you think I came to this office? Hmm? By being unsteady, by being influenced by my wife? By giving in to fears of the imagination? This is serious.

Beat.

This is an important role I have now, and you will see me as the man I am.

Beat.

And you, you will be steady too.
You will stand beside me. Do you understand? And do as I ask.

Nora And what if he does as I fear?

Thomas He won't.

Nora But I asked what if he does.

Thomas All right, if he does, we'll get through it. I am man enough to stand up to the press. I will take it all on my shoulders, all the accusations. It won't concern or hurt you or the children.
You are my wife and my job is to protect you.

Nora Do you mean that?

Thomas Of course I do.

Nora You might not be able to.

Thomas Listen, we'll get through it together, Nora, I promise you, as man and wife.

He comes down to her on the floor.

Nora Say it again.

Thomas You know I will always protect you.

Beat.

Now, stand up, Nora. Act like the politician's wife that you are.

She stands up.
He embraces her.

And don't ever rip my papers again.

Dr Rank comes to the door.

Dr Rank Sorry, I should have knocked.

Thomas pulls away.

Thomas Come in, Dr Rank. We need a distraction. We have a frightened Nora-mouse today, my friend.

Dr Rank Oh really?

Thomas All fired up with imagination.
Can you soothe her and give me a minute before coming through to my office?

Dr Rank Of course I can.

Thomas walks out.
Pause.

What?

Nora Nothing.

Pause.

Dr Rank I know it's not nothing.

Nora We had a disagreement.

Dr Rank I don't want to come between you and Thomas.

Nora And never you would.

Beat.

Dr Rank I may not be the person to cheer you up I'm afraid.

Nora Why not?

Dr Rank Something's wrong, Nora.

Nora Please don't joke, I'm already frightened.

Dr Rank Something is wrong with me.

Nora More bad news.

Beat.

Dr Rank Seems I'm sinking into my grave at the rate of about a foot every other day. I'm probably already knee-deep in England's mud without knowing it and I haven't even bought a plot yet.

Nora Oh, Dr Rank.

Dr Rank Maybe I should ask to be put to sea.

Nora Please don't talk like this.

Dr Rank I'll tell you the way that Thomas would see it. He would do an audit of my internal economy and pronounce me bankrupt. He'd say if I want more time I would have to borrow it.

Pause.

How does one borrow time, Nora?

Nora doesn't know what to say.

And the worst is that one has to live through it. It may last weeks, a month or two at most, but still I have to live through it. I have seen enough others go through it, I can describe the process in detail. The last hours . . .
   Thomas mustn't see it.

I want to ask you that in all seriousness. He's a sensitive soul – underneath the politician's skin there's a little child that when faced with the weakness of the body, recoils. Keep him away, please, once the final disintegration has started.

Nora He'll want to say goodbye.
We both will.

Dr Rank I forbid it.
Ugliness is best kept in private.
Anyway, perhaps the body pays penance for the sins of the past. In my case my free and subaltern youth.
Oh yes, asparagus and foie gras I have eaten.

Nora You don't believe that.

Dr Rank But there are those who do, and who knows? They could be right.
I never should have trusted oysters.

Nora Oysters?

Dr Rank And truffles, truth be known.
Oh indeed, have I eaten truffles.
And all the champagne and port that goes with them.

Nora Indeed.
But it does seem a pity that these delicious things should attack the spine.

Dr Rank Particularly when the poor spine never had the fun of them.

Nora Yes, that is an awful pity.

Dr Rank Hmm.

Nora Hmm.
Why did you smile?

Dr Rank It was you who laughed.

Nora No, it was you who smiled, Dr Rank.

Dr Rank You're a bigger rascal than I thought you were.

Nora Thank God for you, I needed to laugh.

Dr Rank So it seems.

Nora You mustn't go and die on us.

Dr Rank I would like to say that I'll try hard not to.

Nora Then don't.
I'd be so cross with you. Really I would, without you, who would I have?

Beat.
  Dr Rank is perhaps fighting back tears.

Come here, I'll show you something. Might cheer us both up.

Dr Rank What is it?

Nora Part of my costume. For this party we're having.

Dr Rank A party?

Nora Yes, and you must come. It's the Sylvesters' idea.
Thomas wants me to dance.

Dr Rank You know I hate Americans.

Nora It won't just be the Sylvesters, there'll be plenty others, and look –
I've got these for the occasion.

She holds up a pair of stockings.

Dr Rank Silk?

Nora What do you think? No, you can only see the feet. Oh well you might as well see a bit higher up too.
Oh goodness, I don't think they're going to fit. What do you think?

Dr Rank How on earth could I give you an informed opinion about that?

Nora Estimate.

He looks at the stockings, then at her legs.
Nora giggles.

Shame on you.

Dr Rank Shame on you, you started it.

Nora Oh, don't go and die on us.

Dr Rank As I said, I'll try not to.

Nora At least come to the party first.

They giggle again.
She puts the stockings away.

Dr Rank What did Kelman want with you?

Beat.

Nora?

Nora Hmm?

Dr Rank You know what I'm talking about.

Nora He's blackmailing me.

Dr Rank Don't joke.

Nora I'm not joking.

Dr Rank Whatever for?

Beat.

Nora That's the thing about blackmail. I can't say.

Dr Rank You know I'd do anything for you, Nora dear, don't you?
Anything . . . You would just have to name it.

Beat.

Nora Maybe I should . . . maybe telling you would help, maybe you'd be able to find a way through it.

Dr Rank Nora, let me tell you, we have all made mistakes, taken paths that turn out not to be the right ones . . .

Beat.

You must know that I would die rather than leave you with a problem that I couldn't help.

Nora Don't talk about death so lightly.

Dr Rank You are everything to me, Nora, you must know that.

Nora I know that.

Dr Rank More than everything.

Nora Well, either I'm everything or not, I can't be more than everything.

Dr Rank Why else do you think I come to this house every day?

Nora To see my husband.

Dr Rank Thomas? That inflexible toad.

Nora Dr Rank!

Dr Rank Don't pretend you don't know how I look at you.

Nora I'm not pretending.

Dr Rank Nora –

Nora We're friends.

Dr Rank Of course we are. The best. Listen, perhaps I shouldn't say anything, but I told myself that this wasn't a secret to carry to the grave, that I would tell you. And so I will –

Nora Please don't.

Dr Rank But if I don't, I'll still be burdened.

Nora Oh heavens.

Dr Rank I only say this so you know that you can confide in me with total trust.

Nora I have misled you, Dr Rank.

Dr Rank Of course you haven't.

Nora Annie, could we please have some more light in this room?

Dr Rank What's wrong, have I upset you?

Nora Yes, if you want to know, you have upset me very much.

Dr Rank I just want you to feel safe, telling me what you must.

Nora Safe?

Dr Rank Just because I have feelings for you, is that something so awful?

Nora Not in themselves.

Annie comes in.

Dr Rank I'll be dead in two months, I'm not asking anything of you.

Nora Just put the lamps there, please.
It's the fact that you spoke of it.

Dr Rank I didn't, you didn't let me.

Nora You would have done, you were about to.

Dr Rank So it's the speaking of it that offends you?

Nora Yes, because then it's out in the open and we must steer our way around it. I cannot even look you in the eye now, knowing what we both nearly heard you say. You can't take words like that back, Dr Rank.

Dr Rank I didn't actually say it.

Nora It's all ruined between us.

Dr Rank Don't be ridiculous.

Nora You'll have to excuse me.

Dr Rank You aren't going to let me help you?

Nora After this?

Dr Rank You said you were in trouble, now you know I will do whatever I can for you.

Nora But don't you see? After this, I can't ask.

Annie Another lamp, madam?

Nora I think so, Annie, yes please.

Annie Very good.

Dr Rank stands up.

Dr Rank I'll go then, I'm sorry.

Nora No, stay, act just as you did before.

Dr Rank Before what? There was no great declaration, you didn't let me.

Beat.

Annie There's a man here, ma'am.

Dr Rank You need your friends, Nora, don't push me away. You know I could help you.

Annie hands Nora a calling card.

Just say the word. I could leave you my whole fortune, Nora, you know that.

Nora Yes, and create absolute scandal.
You're no help to me now whatsoever. You've ruined any help you might have been.
My husband will be ready to see you now.

Dr Rank comes over to her, quite close.
He kisses her forehead.

Dr Rank Ridiculous stubborn mouse.

Nora withdraws.

Nora Please don't call me that.

Dr Rank I've called you that for years.

Nora Goodbye, Dr Rank.

Dr Rank leaves.

Annie, where is he?

Annie He came up the back stair.

Nora Let him in, but quickly, no one must know he's here.

Nora prepares herself.
Trying to calm herself down, she sits down then changes her mind and stands up.
Kelman comes in, looking worse for wear.

You'll have to speak quietly, my husband's just through that door.

Neil You think I care?

Nora I wasn't able to help you, I tried, I –

Neil Don't lie to me, Mrs Vaughan.

I just had a call from Jacob McGuire, I still have friends, he's been my typist for ten years, after all. He told me about your husband's article.

Nora I begged him not to send it.

Neil When McGuire said he was typing a letter to the press my heart leapt, I would have kissed you then. Mrs Vaughan, I thought, Mrs Vaughan is my salvation. Clever clever woman.

Nora He wouldn't listen.

Neil Then he went on and told me what it said.

Nora HE WOULDN'T LISTEN, DIDN'T YOU HEAR ME?

Neil Well, he is going to have to.

Nora Heaven help me.

Neil You don't have to back away, I'm not going to harm you.

Nora Harm me? You don't know how much you're harming me.

Neil How about this –? No, just hear me out. It hasn't gone to press yet. How about you, I and your husband, we sit down together and see if we can work something out? I have a letter here for Thomas that explains.

Nora He can't ever know, I told you –

Neil How can you stop him? Don't you see you're as trapped as me.

Nora I only have one payment left, I am begging you –

Neil It's immaterial if you can't pay it.
  And anyway, even if you did, frankly, and I'm sorry to say this, I like you, I really do or I might if I knew you,

but even if you did pay me I wouldn't give you your IOU back. What, give away my evidence, my only trump card?

Beat.

You have to understand what it is to be in my shoes.

This is a backstreet loan, Mrs Vaughan, we aren't regulated now.

Nora You know when the others talked about you as this weasel –

Neil Don't call me that.

Nora This broken man with no morals, they said you were base and nasty and a low-life.

Neil You don't know how I've lived.

Nora No, exactly, but I tried to see past it – he has children, I thought to myself, he needs help. I even begged Thomas.

Neil You begged him to save yourself, not me.

Nora True, but I tried to find a little compassion for you.

Neil As I have for you.

Beat.

Nora Tell me how much you're demanding from us. If this is blackmail at least lay down your terms.

Neil I don't want money.

Nora Oh please.

Neil What use is money to me, a few thousand here that will maybe last a year or so, and then what? You'll blacklist me, between the two of you you'll make sure I never work again. I need my career. Politics has been everything to me.

It's going to be a straight fight, him or me.

Nora I won't let that happen.

Neil How can you stop it? I'm sorry to say this, and you don't know how much I regret it, but you're the one with absolutely no choice in all of this.

Nora I have options.

Neil Oh really, what, you're going to throw yourself off a bridge?

Tie your husband's shoelaces together and hang yourself from a door, or under the ice maybe, maybe you'll just swim out in the frozen sea, let yourself go in the cold, black water.

Nora I could.

Neil Be found the next day, washed up, bloated, hairless, unrecognisable.

Nora You don't scare me.

Neil You don't scare me either, Mrs Vaughan.

People like you never see that sort of thing through. Oh, they might threaten it, they might make a great show of telling people that that is what they intend, but see it through? Nah.

Nora I have all kinds of strengths that you don't know about.

Neil It wouldn't do any good anyway. I'd still have your husband by the testicles.

Nora What did you say?

Neil This is no place for drawing-room talk. It's his crotch I've got him by, and you. Think, girl. With you out the way I could do just as much damage to his reputation, I could say he knew all along but covered it up, and you were left to take the blame. That the borrowing was his idea, but the gutless man didn't have the strength to take out a loan in his own name. I will leave this letter for your husband on the way out.

Nora launches herself at him.
He pushes her off.

You don't belong here, Mrs Vaughan, you know. You belong in the sewer with me.

He starts to leave.

Nora Now I have the courage to do it.

Neil So do it, you won't save him that way.

He goes.
She runs over to the door.
A letter falls into Thomas's letterbox.

Nora Oh Lord.

Mrs Lyle comes in by the other door.

Christine Don't sound so full of despair. I've managed to stitch back most of the seams.
   Shall we try it on?

Nora Christine, come here.
   I need you to listen to me.

Christine You're hurting my arm.

Nora If anything should happen to me –

Christine What sort of 'happen'?

Nora I need a witness, that I was of sound mind.

Christine What do you mean, 'sound mind'? You don't seem 'sound' at all.

Nora If I should go mad.

Christine Mad?

Nora Or anything happened to me which meant I wouldn't be here.

Christine You're scaring me now.

Nora Nobody forced me to do anything. I want you to stand as witness, just in case anyone tries to take everything on himself, do you see? All the choices I made were my own. Do you understand?

Will you testify if you need to?

Christine Yes, but I have no idea what you're talking about.

Nora If something extraordinary was going to happen.

Christine What sort of 'extraordinary'?

Nora A sort of a miracle I suppose.

But I don't think it should happen, no, it must never happen.

Christine Kelman was the one who lent you the money, wasn't he?

Don't look at me like that, Nora, do you think I'm completely dim? Of course he did. And now he's blackmailing you, no doubt. I know that because I know him, and he's done all this before.

The man is infuriating. He makes things worse for himself, he's like a snake in a trap, thrashing around. Don't worry, I'll talk to him –

Nora How can you help this?

Christine Nora, don't underestimate me. There was a time when he'd have done anything to help Christine here.

Nora Kelman?

Christine Why is that so surprising?

Nora Because –

Christine Because he's a rat? A weasel?
 No, I don't think so, I think he's a drowning man who's trying to save his life in the only way he knows.
 Where does he live?

Nora feels about in her pockets.
 She finds his card.

Nora I don't think you should go alone.

Christine There may be things I am scared of in this world, Nora, but Neil Kelman is not one of them.

Someone knocks at the door.

Thomas Nora-mouse?

Nora Yes.

Thomas Why have you locked the door?

Nora I . . .

Christine She's trying on her costume, Mr Vaughan.
 And it looks very nice on.
 (*To Nora.*) I don't know the street.

Nora (*to Christine*) It's just around the corner.

Thomas Can't we come in?

Nora (*to Christine*) But his letter is already in the box.

Christine (*to Nora*) Your husband keeps the key?

Nora (*to Christine*) Always.

Christine Just a moment, Mr Vaughan.
 (*To Nora.*) Then we'll get Neil to think of some excuse, and ask for his letter back.

Nora (*to Christine*) But Thomas will check his letterbox any moment.

Christine (*to Nora*) Then it's up to you to distract him.

Beat.

You can do that, can't you?

> *Christine goes.*
> *Nora goes over to her husband's study and opens the door.*

Thomas Well, it comes to something when a man is locked out of his own sitting room.
What, no costume?

Nora Sorry, no.

Thomas We were led to believe there was going to be a marvellous transformation.

> *Rank comes in too.*

Nora Sorry to disappoint.

Dr Rank Nothing to show?

Nora Not until tomorrow.

Thomas You look worn out. Too much practising?

Nora Not enough. I need your help with the steps, actually.

Thomas Fine, but just let me look to see who has sent me a letter.

> *He goes towards the box.*

Nora Please, Thomas, there aren't any in there.

Thomas I can see one from here.

Nora It's not important.

Thomas How do you know, are you part of the cabinet now?

Nora Of course not.

Thomas That could be a very important memo, Nora.

Nora I shan't be able to dance tomorrow if I don't rehearse now.

Thomas Two minutes, that's all.

Nora But say it *is* a memo, and then you'll have to deal with it, and it could involve telephone conversations and letter-writing and a whole deal of worry.
    You said yourself that you needed distracting from it all, and it's Christmas Day.

Thomas It would be neglectful to not read my post.

Dr Rank I think you should listen to her, Thomas.

    Thomas starts to walk towards the box.

Thomas I'll just check it isn't from the Prime Minister, if it is from him it will have his own stamp.

    Nora starts to stamp out a rhythm on the floor. The tarantella.
        It stops Thomas in his tracks.
        He carries on, he gets his letterbox key out.
        She starts to dance.
        It brings him back to her.

All right, you can dance first.
    But then straight after.

    He stamps his foot as well. As does Dr Rank. Between them they create the rhythm.
        She dances.
        Stately at first, then more wildly, faster and faster.
        Totally out of control.
        Thomas eventually stops her.

Nora, you will make yourself sick.

Nora I want to go on.

Thomas You were dancing as if your life depended on it.

She still dances.

I can't believe you're dancing like this, it's as if you've lost all grace, all elegance, all the things we worked on.

Nora I need some more instruction.

Thomas You certainly do.

Nora You must promise me that you'll go on teaching me right up to the last minute, I don't want to make a fool of myself.

Thomas I think I'll have to.

Nora Don't even take a break to do anything, no work, nothing.

Thomas You mustn't be so jealous Nora, you know I must work.

Nora But on Christmas Day.

Dr Rank I wouldn't risk upsetting her any further.

Thomas All right, no letters today.

Dr Rank If it were from the Prime Minister it would have come with something for you to sign.

Thomas Are you sure?

Nora Or tomorrow.
No letters tomorrow.

Thomas What?

Nora Not until my dance is done.

Beat.
Thomas looks at Dr Rank. Dr Rank raises his eyebrows – as if to say, you had better let her have it her way.

Thomas All right! Talk about browbeaten, I am entirely yours.

But tomorrow night, after the party I am the cabinet minister once more, and I will have to read what I have been sent.

Annie comes in.

Annie Dinner is served, madam.

Nora We will have champagne, Annie.

Annie Very good.

Thomas A feast?!

Nora And macaroons, Annie, please, lots of them.

Dr Rank (*to Thomas*) She isn't . . . ?

Thomas What?

Dr Rank Well, you know . . .

Thomas Not as far as I know. Just Nora, being Nora as ever.

Dr Rank Strange little mouse you have there.

Thomas Very strange.

They go offstage.
Christine comes back in.

Nora ?

Christine I had to leave a note, he wasn't there.

Nora Maybe it is better to let things take their own course. Maybe this is where my life has been headed after all. And maybe, just maybe this is what we've needed. Maybe a miracle is going to occur in this very house.

Christine What miracle?

Nora Thomas.

Maybe my Tom is going to be miraculous.
It's got to be a possibility, hasn't it?

Christine Of course it has.

Nora Men and women being honest with each other, sorting things out. You read about it in books.

Christine I certainly believe in it.

Nora Come on, let's please go to dinner.

It's seven o'clock, five hours to midnight, then another twenty-four until the dance. That's thirty-one in total. Thirty-one hours, then it's all over one way or the other.

Christine Let me wipe your face, Nora, your make-up has run.

Nora lets her.

Nora Don't fuss.

Christine You need to look quite composed. And as you say, there are thirty-one hours, so what else is there to do now but be quite yourself?

She puts her arm through the arm of her friend and they go to dinner.

Act Three

Boxing Day evening.

Upstairs, the Vaughans are having a party. Music can be heard throughout the house.

Mrs Lyle is sitting waiting in the Vaughans' drawing room.

Soft footsteps on the stairs.

She whispers.

Christine Come in.

Neil Kelman comes in, quietly.

Neil Where are they?

Christine Upstairs, we'll have to be quiet.

Neil I don't know what you're playing at, why you brought me here. I wouldn't put it past Thomas for this to be some part of his plan.

Christine I said quiet.

Neil They won't hear anything.

Christine I sent the note.

Neil I know, it said you did.

Christine It was me and me alone.

Neil Why?

Beat.

Christine Lots of reasons. And you.

Neil Don't make me laugh.

Christine There's more to be said between us.

Neil No, I think you said it quite adequately at the time. If you think you've brought me here for some kind of –

Christine I regret what I did.

Neil Well, that makes both of us.

Beat.

What the hell is that music?

Christine The Sylvesters got them to organise a gathering.

Neil With music?

Christine Everyone knows the Vaughans like to dance.

Neil Shame it's at my funeral.
I can see why you're friends with them. You and them suit each other.

Christine Please don't think I'm a heartless ageing woman.

Neil Give me an alternative, Mrs Lyle?
How else am I to interpret what you did to me?

Christine You have to see it from my point of view.

Neil What is that? I need some funds, so time to ditch the old flame and start again with the new money?

Christine I had my mother and two brothers to support.

Neil And I was in love.

Beat.

Christine So was I.

Neil Yeah, with yourself.

Christine Not true.

Beat.

Neil I don't think you can have been in love in the way that I was. The way I felt about you – well, no amount of needing money or pragmatism would have come between us. I would have done anything for you, gone anywhere. All my waking moments were filled with you, and the nights, the nights I ached for you because you weren't beside me.

Beat.

Yeah well, anyway.

Christine You wouldn't believe me if I said it was the same for me.

Neil It might be nice to hear.

Christine That every single day I regret what I did. That I know I ruined my own life and yours too.

Neil I would love to believe you.
    Unfortunately I can't. Not a single word.
    I hate you, Christine, if you want to know.
    You have become the person in this world I least wanted to see again. And to see you here in this place, yes it's fitting. I've heard you have a job with him now too, well, that doesn't surprise me either.

Christine I still love you.

Beat.

Neil For Christ's sake.

Beat.
    He looks at her.
    Beat.

I've screwed the Vaughans.

Christine I know you have.

Neil And before, you heard about what I did before?

Christine I heard the allegations.

Neil They're true.

Christine I thought they might be.

Neil I had to sign, I was up to my neck in it, it was a way I thought I could be free.

Christine I wish I'd been by your side, all these years.

Neil I could have done with it.
  Probably.

Christine We might have fallen out.

Neil I doubt it.

Christine By now. We'd have been sick of the sight of each other. Three or more children down, and up to our ears in debt for the small house we owned.

Neil It sounds nice.

  Beat.

But politics became everything after you left me. That was all I had.
  And I'm not going to lose it now.

Christine You will get your seat back.

Neil Don't make me laugh.

Christine You just have to know how to handle these things.

Neil I don't think you know what you're talking about.

Christine You'd be surprised, I know a thing or two about the world.
  I have a small flat I've just taken a lease out on, I have a table, and two chairs, a single bed and a chest of drawers. I have a small salary, if I get the job. If not, I'll try somewhere else.

Neil Why are you telling me this?

Christine Because you need rescuing.

Beat.

Neil Oh, I'm with you, I'm with you now. She put you up to this, I should have seen it coming. Of course, this is the length you'll go to to save your friend, you're all the same, you women –

Christine I threw away my life once for someone else's sake, I'm not going to do it again.
I've missed you, Neil, every single day.

Neil I don't know whether to listen to you, or run out of the door.
Are you joking, are you some cruel apparition? Did I drink at lunchtime?

She takes his hand.

Christine You are shaking.

Neil I wept for you. My wife, my poor dear wife, whom I tried to love, she said I used to call the name Christine in my sleep.

Christine Here I am.

He holds her by the shoulders.

Neil If you're teasing me –

Christine No tease.

He kisses her.

Neil So laugh at me.

Christine I'm not laughing.

He kisses her a second time.

Neil I'm a bad man, you know that, I've done some terrible things.

Christine That's why you need me.

He kisses her again.

Neil What about the Vaughans?

Christine I think you should leave them alone, no more demands. Admit defeat.

Beat.

Thomas can't give you what you want, and Nora can't make him.
   I know it's painful, but –

Neil My letter?

Christine Well, yesterday I'd have said, go upstairs and find Thomas, demand it back, then shake his hand and go, but today . . .

Neil I can do that of course.

Christine No, don't. Today I think something different, I've seen things.

Neil Do you know what you're saying?

Christine Leave the letter where it is.

Neil She said it would kill him.

Christine She doesn't know what good men are capable of. They need to talk it through, those two, she can't continue keeping this secret from him, and he has to accept what she did, she did for him.

Neil Are you sure?

Christine Yes, they'll go nowhere otherwise.
   And they love each other, after all.

He kisses her again.

Neil I didn't realise that I wasn't alive.

And again.

All these years I've been dead.

Beat.

But my boys –
I have two boys, is there enough room in your flat for my two boys?

Christine I love children.

Neil They're a little more than children.

Christine I'm sure I will love them whatever their size.

Neil Are you sure, playing mother to someone else's offspring?

Christine We'll have to go out in the morning and buy some more chairs. That's all.

He smiles.

Neil Can I kiss you again?

Christine You have already four times, I don't see why you should have to ask.

He kisses her again.

Neil I might not be able to stop.

Christine Then don't.
Except, I hear a door opening, it sounds like they're coming down.

Neil I'll wait for you outside, at the end of the road.

Christine Yes, do, then walk me home. See the chair situation for yourself.

He comes back and kisses her again and again.

Neil, you have to go.

> *He kisses her one more time, then goes.*
> *Mrs Lyle, alone, puts her fingers to her lips, remembering his kiss.*
> *Then she picks up her hat and coat.*
> *She is putting them on when Nora and Thomas come through the door.*
> *They don't see her at first.*

Nora Did we have to come down so early?

Thomas The party is nearly over.

Nora We must have appeared rude.

Thomas Everyone was tired.

Nora But they were still dancing.

Thomas Let them. We can dance too. Down here. Alone. Or I can dance, you can be quite still.

> *Mrs Lyle coughs to make her presence known.*

Nora Christine!

Christine Good evening.

Thomas So it is.

Christine Forgive me, but having helped mend the costume, I did want to see it on.

Nora Well, here it is.

Christine You look exquisite, truly wonderful.

Thomas Now you have seen it.

Christine So I have.

Nora Shall I do another twirl for you?

Thomas A quick one.

Nora does another twirl.

Nora But she can't really see in this light.

Thomas She can see perfectly well.

Nora I want her to see how the costume glimmers.

Thomas You can see the glimmers, can't you, Mrs Lyle?

Christine I –

Nora Would you fetch some candles, Thomas, please? You really should have come up, seen it for yourself.

Christine I wouldn't have dreamed of it.

Beat.

Nora Candles, please.

Thomas It's past midnight, I thought we were going to bed.

Nora A few moments, that's all.

Thomas Very well.

He goes off to get some candles.
Nora and Mrs Lyle have a few seconds to talk, alone.

Nora Well?

Christine You're going to have to tell him everything.

Nora I knew it.

Christine I think Kelman will back off, but his letter is still there.

Nora Heaven help me.

Christine It won't be as bad as you think.

Nora Are you in your right mind?

Christine Trust him, Nora.

Nora Hush, he's coming back. Oh, Christine, thank you for trying.

Christine You have to trust him, let him help you. Stop being so modern.

Thomas comes back in with candles.

Thomas There you go. Now, if you've finished admiring her –
It really is late, I don't mean to be rude.

Christine Of course, I'm just going.

Thomas Thank you so much.

Thomas is ushering her out.

Christine Goodbye, Nora.

Nora Goodbye, Christine.

Thomas closes the door on her.

Thomas Damn.

Nora What?

Thomas She's forgotten her knitting.

Nora I'm not surprised, the speed with which you tried to get her out of the room.

Thomas Am I not allowed to want to be alone with you?

Nora Of course.

Thomas She can come back for it tomorrow, no doubt she'll be back tomorrow.

Nora Aren't you tired, Thomas?

Thomas Not at all.

Nora Not even a little bit sleepy?

Thomas Surely you aren't going cold on me, are you? After all that dancing, I'd have thought your blood would be racing. I know mine is.

Nora I think the dance has exhausted me.

Thomas Then let me wake you up.
  You know you're irresistible this evening, don't you?

Nora I think I just need to sleep.

Thomas And deny me the chance to enjoy all this loveliness? All evening I was looking over to you, and thinking, she's all mine. I own all that. I was pretending that it was our first evening together, and later we would come back here, and I would peel off your clothes gently, very gently, one by one, as if I was the first person to ever touch you – why are you backing away? More tarantella in your blood?

Nora Haven't you heard me at all?

Thomas Yes I have heard you, but then why dance? Why go to all that effort if not to please me.

Nora I enjoy dancing.

Thomas And I enjoy you.
  You know the effect it will have on me, and yet you danced. So now, we dance together.

Nora Thomas.

Thomas Don't tell me you're going to resist me? That only makes my blood boil even more.
  Twelve months I've had the memory of you last year, in that dress, to keep me warm, now here you are in front of me again.
  The tarantella girl.

He grabs her, playfully.
   He kisses her.

Kiss me back.

She kisses him.

Kiss me as if you mean it.

Nora I don't mean it, not tonight when I'm tired.

Thomas Tired? Aren't I your husband?
   Or does the tarantella girl want to fight?

He is grabbing her a little too roughly. She starts to push him away, he only grabs her all the harder.

Nora What's got into you?

Thomas What's got into me? What's got into you?

Nora You hurt my lip.

Someone knocks at the door.
   He lets go of his grip.
   Nora moves away from him, sorts herself out. She dabs at her lip with her finger.
   Thomas goes to the door.
   It is Dr Rank.

Thomas How extremely wonderful to see you.

Dr Rank comes in.

Dr Rank And you too.

Thomas No really, what an excellent time of night for a visit, how thoughtful you are.

Beat.

Dr Rank Well, I just thought I'd put my head around the door, say goodnight.

Thomas Of course you did.

97

Nora Come in, Dr Rank.

Dr Rank I thought I could smell cigar smoke.

Thomas None here.

Dr Rank Then I'm mistaken, forgive me.

Beat.

Fine, I won't keep you. I was just going to thank you for the party. And I had some tests done today, your wife asked me to tell her the results so I thought I'd keep my promise.

Nora And what were the results?

Dr Rank The best.

Nora Good news?

Dr Rank Excellent.

Nora Wonderful!

Dr Rank Certainty. That is what they were.

Nora Certainty?

Dr Rank Absolute certainty for both doctor and patient.

Nora That doesn't sound good.

Dr Rank Now if you will excuse me –
I need to take off my costume and get home.

Thomas Very good.

Nora Won't you stay a while?
Talk about all the costumes that were there, and who we might all come as next year.

Dr Rank Next year is easy.

Nora Oh really?

Dr Rank Yes, you shall go as Lady Luck.

Thomas How will she do that?

Dr Rank Oh, she'll just have to dress in her own clothes.

Thomas Very nicely put.
And you? What will you be?

Dr Rank Next year I'll be invisible.

Thomas That's a funny idea.

Dr Rank There's a big black cloak – haven't you heard of the cloak of invisibility? – that comes right down over you, and then you can't see anyone any more and no one can see you.

Nora gasps.
Thomas laughs.

Thomas What a strange mood you're in. He's joking, Nora, don't take him seriously.
Here, have a cigar.

He reaches for the cigar box.

Dr Rank Thank you. I'll smoke it on my way home.

Thomas A fine idea.

Nora Don't go just yet.

Dr Rank I think I must.

Nora Sleep well then, Dr Rank.

Dr Rank A pretty thought.

Nora And wish the same for me.

Dr Rank You? All right, if you want to . . . sleep well.

He brushes her hand with his.
Then he goes.

Thomas Drunk as a lord.

Nora Very probably.

Something drops into the letterbox.

Thomas Whatever is he doing that for?
He's put something into our letterbox.

Nora Has he?

Thomas There's something not right with him today,
despite his good news.

Thomas reaches for the keys to his letterbox.

And before you say anything, I just want to see what he's
up to.
Someone's been at this lock.

Nora Really?

Thomas One of your hairpins, Nora.

Nora Must have been the children.

Thomas Well, make sure they don't do it again.

He opens it.

Two visiting cards, from Dr Rank.
Silly fool, does he think we don't know his address?
Hang on, he's put a black cross above his name, look
at this. It's almost as if he's announcing his own funeral.

Nora I think he is.

Thomas What?

Nora He's very ill. Terminally ill.

Thomas He didn't say anything to me. Are you sure?

Nora I'm afraid I am.

Thomas Rank, near death?

Nora nods.

I can't believe it. Why would he tell you and not me?

Nora He didn't want to distress you.

Thomas Then we must hold each other all the more tightly, Nora.
How awful for him.

Beat.

Nora You need to read your letters now.

She reaches into the box and gives a letter to him.

It's from Neil Kelman.

Beat.
He takes it.

Thomas Good gracious.

Nora I'll leave you to it.

Thomas No, I want you here.

Nora I need to go to bed.

Thomas Stay with me a few more moments.

Thomas opens it.

Whatever Kelman has to say to me, we said we would face it together.
But anyway the man is full of hot air, he . . .

Thomas reads.
Nora stays quite still.
She looks at him once.
Then the floor.

Nora I'm sorry, I can't bear this, I have to . . . I'm sorry, I –

Thomas STAY EXACTLY WHERE YOU ARE.

She is pinned to the spot.
    Thomas continues to read.
    Then he deliberately puts the letter away back in the
envelope.

Nora Let me go.

Thomas Where are you going?

Nora You mustn't try and save me.

Thomas Save you?

Nora It's the only way, you must let me go.

Thomas Is it true?

Beat.

IS IT TRUE?

Nora Yes, it's true.

Thomas Good God.

Nora I loved you more than anything else, that's the truth.

Thomas Don't even think about trying to win me over
with your words.

Nora I had to take you away, if anyone had seen you in
that state –

Thomas I had pneumonia.

Nora I think you almost believe that.

Thomas I was ill, yes, but would have recovered.

Nora You were insane.

Thomas OF COURSE I WASN'T.
    Never use that word.

Nora You were a danger to yourself.

Thomas Miserable woman, do you know what you have done?

Nora Are you even listening?

Thomas They will drag you through the mud, do you realise that? You think Kelman's had a hard time? You? You will be hung out to dry. Do you understand me? Do you know how bad it's going to get for you?

Nora Yes, I'm starting to understand –

Thomas Stop play-acting. You are staying here to give an account of yourself. What the hell were you thinking?

Nora I was trying to protect you.

Thomas With fraud? A fraud allegation, this is protecting me?

Nora I had to take you away.

Thomas Not like this.

Nora There was no other way to get the money.

Thomas Don't, don't come near me. I don't want to hear a justification of this.
    This is the end of everything, you realise that? We are ruined.

Nora It is me, not you.

Thomas It reflects on me. I should have known when I married you that you were too good to be true, there was all that stuff about your father, but I turned a blind eye.

Nora Don't bring my father into this.

Thomas Why not? – That's obviously where you get your low morals from.

Beat.

You do understand what you've done to me, to us?
  Say yes if you've heard me.

Nora Yes.

Thomas Then we have to think how we can appease
him. Ask him what he's wanting – whatever happens we
have to hush this thing up, whatever the cost, you hear
me? We'll sell everything we have if that's what it takes.
I will not have my reputation ruined. Oh, take that damn
shawl off, would you, I can hardly bear to look at you.

  She takes her shawl off.

Nora You said we would stand together.

Thomas And we will. In public.
  In private, well, what? You expect me to go on as
before? See you as the same woman I did? You're a
criminal, Nora. What you did, well, it's punishable with a
prison sentence. I'll protect you from the courts, if I can,
but here . . .
  We'll live together as man and wife, at least as far as
everyone outside this house is concerned. You'll still play
your public roles, but inside these four walls things will
be rather different.
  The children for a start. I cannot allow you to raise the
children. I'll find a good governess, and trust her with the
task. You've said goodbye to happiness, you know that,
both our happiness. You'll live in this house as I feel fit.
In a room of your own. With the servants if I decide.

  The doorbell rings.

Who the hell can be calling at this hour?
  Don't move, Nora, you stay there. I'll go and see who
it is.
  If anyone asks for you, I'll say you are not well.

Maybe it's best of all that you be totally hidden from now on.

Nora stays where she is.
 Thomas goes to the door.
 Annie appears with a note.

Who was it, Annie?

Annie Someone with a note for Mrs Vaughan.

Thomas Pass it to me, Annie, please.

Annie hands it to Thomas.

You may go.

Nora holds out a hand.

Don't think you'll get to read your own post now either.

Nora You cannot treat me this way.

Thomas You are my wife, Nora, I will treat you as I want.

He opens it.

Nora!
 Nora.
 You won't believe it.

Nora What is it?

Thomas Something incredible.
 Truly incredible.

He holds out the IOU.

We've been given another chance!

Nora The IOU?

Thomas He has returned it, with a polite note saying he will not trouble us any further. Good God, I can't believe it, the relief. It hasn't happened, Nora, the nightmare. It didn't happen. He's sent it back. Oh my sweet, I can't tell you how relieved I am. Come here, let me embrace you.

Nora Embrace me?

Thomas You don't understand, it's over. We've been through the most awful time, but it's behind us. It didn't happen. Oh let me touch you, my dear heart, it's behind us.

Nora Don't touch me.

Thomas What do you mean? He has sent his IOU back.

Nora We're free from Kelman, yes.

Thomas So we are totally free.

Nora But something else has happened here tonight.

Thomas Don't dwell on what I said just now, I was furious. I wasn't thinking. I've forgiven you, really, it's all all right. I see that you can't bring yourself to believe it, but it's true, I have forgiven you totally and utterly. Isn't that wonderful?

Beat.

You loved me as a wife should love a husband, it was simply that you didn't have the experience to know what you were doing – but you think I love you any less for that? On the contrary, I love you even more, knowing that I must protect and look after you, and honestly I find your naivety quite attractive. I'll let you lean on me, whenever and always.

Nora Annie.

Thomas What are you doing?

Nora ANNIE.

Annie comes to the door.

Please bring in my day dress and my coat.

Thomas Your coat?

Annie Very good.

Annie has gone.

Thomas What are you doing?

Nora I am leaving you.

Thomas What?

Nora You heard me. I will be gone inside the hour.

Thomas You aren't thinking straight – I said I've forgiven you.

Nora I can't live here, Thomas.

Thomas This is your home.

Nora This is your home, and I just live here. No, it isn't even your home, it belongs to the government. Everything is about the politician, and nothing about the man. And I have tried. I have bent myself to your wishes. I have tried to be the wife you want me to be, and when I do the one thing I'm proud of, the one time I really did something, you throw it back in my face.

Thomas It was fraud.

Nora I WAS SAVING YOU.
    You can't even hear it, can you, because you can't look the fact that you needed saving in the face and say, yes, and thank you.

Beat.

Thomas ANNIE, she doesn't need her coat.

Nora Yes, I do, and my dress, I'll pay for them both as soon as I get on my feet.

Thomas I said I'd forgiven you, didn't you hear?

Nora I don't need your forgiveness, Thomas, can't *you* hear?

I was acting as a wife should.

Thomas And I love you for it.

Nora No, you don't love me. If you loved me – God, Thomas, if you had loved me, we'd have sat here ten minutes ago and tried to work it out together, which by the way is exactly what in a moment of prowess you promised. If you loved me, you'd have begged in thankfulness, not once but a thousand times for what I did for you. Don't you think I knew it was risky? Don't you think I knew I was playing with fire to go anywhere near Kelman and his dirty backstreet loans? I did it, Thomas, because, strangely, I did love you. Or thought I did.

Thomas And I love you, I swear.

Nora You don't know what it is, even.

The more you say you love me, the more I realise you have no real understanding. To love someone, Thomas, you'd lay down anything for them. You'd risk reputation, imprisonment, death itself, anything to save them, with no thought of the consequences for yourself or your blessed political career.

Thomas No one risks that.

You know what politics is like.

Nora But I did.

Don't you see? I risked it all.

Beat.

Thomas We can rebuild, Nora, we can start again, I realise I said a few things I shouldn't have, I went too far, I always do.

Nora We don't have anything to start with, not even a basis.

You haven't ever made any attempt to know me. What I like, what I don't like, even whether or not I want to make love on a particular evening. You needed a wife, a family, because it gave you something that people could trust, that was for outside these doors, and inside, it was all right as long as you could touch me when you wanted. And me, I haven't helped, I've lived like a beggar in this house, begging you for money or for furnishings. No, a prostitute, that's what I've been.

Thomas Don't be ridiculous –

Nora I've lived off the fact that you wanted me.
And when you wanted me, I could ask you for things. If that isn't harlotry, then what is?

Thomas You sound ungrateful, you've been happy here.

Nora Yes, but I was mistaken.
I thought I was happy, but I was wrong.

Nora puts on her coat.

Thomas Think of the scandal, Nora, please.

Nora The scandal?
The scandal is here, in front of me.

She starts to walk towards the door.

Thomas You are a mother and a wife, first and foremost.

Nora First and foremost I am myself – Nora. I will miss them, yes, but –

He runs and stands between her and the door.

Thomas You are ill, delirious, you have talked this evening of insanity.

Nora I have never felt so well.

Thomas Do you love me so little?

Nora I don't love you at all, not now.

Thomas The children then?
    What about the children?

Nora You know I love the children more than life itself, which is why I'm not taking this lightly. But already I've started to train Emmy in the wrong ways. They need to learn from other people, not me. A miracle should have happened here tonight, Thomas, and when it didn't –

Thomas What miracle?

Nora I've explained it now several times. If you still don't understand then there's nothing more I can say.

Thomas I won't move.

Nora You will, Thomas, because you will gain nothing by standing there.

    Beat.
        He doesn't move.

Thomas Wait until the morning . . .?

Nora And spend another night with a stranger? No.

Thomas It's gone midnight and it's freezing out there.

Nora Thomas, please stand aside.

Thomas Couldn't you go on living here with me, as brother and sister?

Nora You know that would never last.
    Please move out of my way.

    He tries to put his arms around her waist.

Thomas Please, Nora, I'm begging you –

Nora Let go, Thomas.
    Thomas?

    He clings on to her, like a child.

Here's your ring. Give me back mine too.

Thomas Never.

Nora Then keep it, but know that I've absolved you of all responsibilities. And I will feel no obligation to you either. I'll leave the keys on the table as I go out.

Thomas How can you be so cold?

Beat.

Nora I don't know, Thomas, and that's the strangest thing.
I'll send for my things, and I'll write to the children.
But you, I'll say goodbye to.

Thomas Can I ever be more than a stranger to you again?

Beat.
She looks at him.

Nora I don't believe in miracles any more, Thomas. And neither should you.
Let go of my coat.

He lets go of her coat.

Goodbye, Mr Vaughan.

She walks out of the door.
Thomas crumples.
He listens for the door.

Thomas Nora? You haven't gone . . . Is this the miracle . . .?

He hears the front door slam behind her.